I0335234

THE ANGEL WHO LOST HER WINGS

Bahareh Amidi

The Angel Who Lost Her Wings

Baharak

ISBN 978-0-9974573-8-4
cover and interior illustrations by
Sara Nikforouz

email: connect@bahareh.com
facebook.com/Bahareh.Amidi
twitter.com/BaharehAmidi
youtube.com/baharehLIVE
instagram.com/bahareh_poetess
www.Bahareh.com

Listen to
The Angel Who Lost Her Wings

One day I finally knew I was here.

Here and Now

Once upon a time there was an Angel.

An Angel who lost her wings.

She was walking through life

wondering what fault

had made her
wings disappear

She saw the birds flying in the sky

and the bees buzzing around

She saw a rock by
the river and sat,
and sat, and sat.

After years of sitting
She decided to walk again
and look for her wings
That is when she started
to fly wingless with heart

Listen to

The Angel Who Lost Her Wings

www.ingramcontent.com/pod-product-compliance
Lightning Source LLC
Chambersburg PA
CBHW040753020526
44118CB00042B/2937
9780997457384